floral
embroidery

Create 10 beautiful modern embroidery projects inspired by nature

For my grandmothers,
who taught me that the act of creation, the breath of nature
and the love of literature is in our blood.
You are wise. You are beautiful. You are my heart.

"With mirth and laughter let old wrinkles come."

The Merchant of Venice, William Shakespeare

floral
embroidery

Create 10 beautiful modern embroidery
projects inspired by nature

TEAGAN OLIVIA STURMER

*Photographs by Jesse Wild
and Riley Fields*

WHITE OWL

First published in Great Britain in 2020 by
PEN & SWORD WHITE OWL
An imprint of Pen & Sword Books Ltd
Yorkshire – Philadelphia

ISBN 9781526759580

Group Publisher: Jonathan Wright
Series Editor and Publishing Consultant: Katherine Raderecht
Photography: Jesse Wild and Riley Fields
Art Director: Jane Toft
Editor: Katherine Raderecht
Stylist: Jaine Bevan

Printed and bound in India, by Replika Press Pvt. Ltd.

Pen & Sword Books Ltd incorporates the Imprints of Pen & Sword Books Archaeology, Atlas, Aviation, Battleground, Discovery, Family History, History, Maritime, Military, Naval, Politics, Railways, Select, Transport, True Crime, Fiction, Frontline Books, Leo Cooper, Praetorian Press, Seaforth Publishing, Wharncliffe and White Owl.

For a complete list of Pen & Sword titles please contact:

PEN & SWORD BOOKS LIMITED
47 Church Street, Barnsley, South Yorkshire S70 2AS, England
E-mail: enquiries@pen-and-sword.co.uk
Website: www.pen-and-sword.co.uk
or
PEN AND SWORD BOOKS
1950 Lawrence Rd, Havertown, PA 19083, USA
E-mail: Uspen-and-sword@casematepublishers.com
Website: www.penandswordbooks.com

contents

introduction

"To thine own self be true, and it must follow, as the night the day,
thou canst not then be false to any man."
Hamlet, William Shakespeare

I want to thank you for picking my book off the bookshelf. Whatever it was that drew you to it, I hope you enjoy reading it and, as you browse through the words and pictures, that it inspires your creative soul. I believe everyone is creative and before you start reading, I want to share with you where my inspiration for this book and my designs come from.

It all starts with a memory of a night spent with my Oma (the German word for grandma). The fire was crackling in the cast iron grate, I was wrapped up in a large handmade quilt and Oma sat across from me, piles of patterned flannel fabric strewn across her lap. Her long fingers cut a piece of thread and she passed it through the eye of her needle.

"Whatever we do, we must create," she said. "Be it quilting, or writing or painting, we are creative beings. All of us. And we must create."

Tying a knot at the end of her thread, she reached down and continued stitching across the red flannel fabric, binding together the layers of the quilt. I will never forget her words. I have turned them into my mantra to live by. We must create. We must always create.

However it was writing, not embroidery, that was my first creative outlet. In my teenage years, I would hole myself up in my bedroom for hours, scribbling down my stories with an old pencil. My characters went on epic adventures through lands that time forgot and imaginary places I had travelled to in my dreams. I also discovered a love for William Shakespeare when, as a child, I found my mother's old college copy of Hamlet. I was immediately seduced by his language, his characters and his wonderful storytelling. Shakespeare's work talked to my soul and also gave me my lifelong love of theatre.

It wasn't until I was grown-up, married and living hundreds of miles away from my family, that I took up embroidery. My mother had bought me an embroidery kit featuring a cat when I was eight or nine and I hated it! Not because I hated the design, but because I didn't want to follow someone else's pattern. I wanted to learn to create my own patterns, make up my own rules, discover the skill in my own way. And that's exactly what I did when I started creating my own embroidery designs as an adult.

The inspiration for my embroidery designs started with my love of flowers. I wanted to learn how to stitch beautiful pink peonies and brilliant yellow sunflowers. Believe me when I say, that my first piece of embroidery was neither beautiful nor brilliant. It was a mess! However, I remembered what my Oma had said, "we must create." And so I kept going, stitch after stitch, mess after mess. I can't tell you the number of designs I had to throw away, fabric I ruined, or thread that was wasted. But I kept going, I kept creating. I had to.

But why was it flowers that I wanted to stitch? That came from my other grandmother, my Grandma Juanita. Her garden stretched alongside the big, red barn out behind my grandparent's house. Rows of cabbages, cucumbers, tomatoes, corn and beans kept the bees busy in the summertime, and our bellies full in the winter. But it was Grandma's flowers that were always the talk of the local county fairs. She would enter her huge red roses into every flower competition and always came home with the blue winner's ribbon. Growing flowers was her passion. She would take me into her garden and teach me about her flowers. Flamboyant roses, sunflowers as large as the span of her hands and peonies that smelled like sweet perfume.

When Grandma Juanita wasn't outside, bent over her flowers, she was inside quilting animal shapes or painting woodland creatures on her furniture. She loved nature in all its forms and she was also very creative. She could quilt, crochet, paint and sew like no one else I knew. But it was her magical flower garden that was her greatest pride and joy. At her funeral a few years ago, an old recording of her singing "Where The Roses Never Fade" was played. In that moment I vowed to carry on Grandma Juanita's legacy by immortalising her beautiful flowers in thread.

This book brings together my passion for embroidery, flowers and Shakespeare and I owe it all to my two grandmothers. Both different, but beautiful and creative in their unique ways. I hope this book inspires you to create too. I want to teach you how to stitch my designs and be inspired to create your own designs too. Pieces that speak to your soul. So let's dig in shall we? After all, we must always create.

HOW THIS BOOK WORKS

I've created this book with one thought in mind. Simplicity. I hope I have accomplished that. Before you start the patterns, I have created an easy guide for finding and choosing the right materials (see Materials). Having the right supplies and tools is extremely important when crafting embroidery pieces, so make sure to read through that chapter very carefully before going out and selecting your materials.

Secondly, you will find a complete guide to stitches (see Stitching Guide). In this chapter, the diagrams and photographs illustrate how to make the stitches you will need to create the patterns. I suggest practicing these stitches on separate pieces of fabric first to get the hang of them before starting the patterns.

I have then created ten patterns designed to take you from the simplest of stitches, to a more complex combination of all the stitches. That way you can grow your stitching skills naturally. With each design, you will find a Shakespeare quote that inspired the embroidery pattern. I hope they offer inspiration to you as well. Once you have finished the patterns, you will find a chapter to help you display your design (see Finishing Your Hoop). A few of the patterns come with some extra fun ideas to add to the finished piece.

Once you have finished all the patterns, the last chapter of this book will guide you through creating your own patterns (see Create Your Own Patterns). Here I talk about colour matching, choosing the right fabrics and learning how to create the textures I use when I make my patterns.

I hope you find inspiration in my book and enjoy your hand embroidery journey!

chapter one: materials

It can feel a bit overwhelming when you start shopping for all the materials you need to start your embroidery hobby. Although it has taken me a few years to collect all the things in this list, they are all easy to find and relatively affordable.

I find these little cardboard bobbins make organising your threads really easy. You can find them in most sewing or craft shops and online and they are very good value.

ESSENTIAL MATERIALS, SUPPLIES AND TIPS

This is a list of all the supplies you need to make the patterns in this book.

FABRIC

My first choice of fabric is linen. It is what I have used to stitch all the patterns in this book and I recommend you do the same. I specifically use a hopsack linen which is a more loosely woven and coarse fabric. Linen is stocked in almost every craft or fabric store and provides a beautiful texture that showcases my floral patterns beautifully. Other fabrics that would also work well are cotton or velvet, which is slightly more difficult to work with. Feel free to use fabric in whatever colour you prefer - this book is, after all, about creative inspiration - but I have designed each pattern's colour palette to work best on white fabric, so that is what I recommend.

THREAD

Embroidery thread, or floss, is also available at almost every craft store. I have found the best quality floss is DMC embroidery thread. For every pattern I list each DMC embroidery thread you will need by its colour code (usually a set of three or four numbers). Of course, you can pick whatever colours you like, but use my recommended colours if you want to follow my patterns exactly.

Embroidery thread is made up of six separate tiny strands. For most of these patterns I suggest you split them into a smaller number of strands to give your embroidery piece different textures. If I suggest separating your strand of floss into two groups of three, or into a 'half split cut', you will simply need to separate your cut of floss in half. It is quite simple.

NEEDLES

The best needles are ones created specifically for embroidery. I tend to use the DMC brand of embroidery needle too. That doesn't mean you can't use sewing needles you already have in your kit, but check the gauges, or sizes, of each needle are the same as stated in my patterns.

I suggest choosing a coarse white linen for all my projects to give a fresh contemporary look to the finished design

My husband made me these great embroidery hoop racks from bits of wood we just had lying around. I use them to store all my hoops out of the way. Simplicity is key!

In some of my patterns, I suggest you need to use different gauge needles for different parts of the design. You might need a 5 gauge for more delicate sections and a 3 gauge needle for areas of the design where you need to use six strands of embroidery thread. However, if you want to use just one needle for the duration of the pattern and aren't sure what size needle it is that you have, that's fine! They key thing to remember is that the higher the gauge number, the smaller the needle. The only time you will need a 3 gauge needle is when you use all six strands of thread, usually for roses, lazy daisy stitches or large French knots.

HOOPS

All the patterns in this book have been created to stitch using a six inch hoop (15.2 x 15.2 cm). This is the most common size for embroidery hoops, and they can be found in almost every craft store. I recommend bamboo or any type of wooden hoop. They are more reliable and more sustainable than plastic hoops. The most important thing is to make sure you keep the tension in your hoop is as tight as possible while you are working on your embroidery piece. You need to be constantly checking that your fabric is pulled taunt in the hoop and adjusting the tightness with the screw when necessary. Pull the fabric tight so there are no puckers. If you don't keep an eye on your hoop tension, your fabric can get crumpled and your stitches will start to become uneven and sloppy.

TRANSFERRING PATTERNS

This step is incredibly easy. Every time you start a new pattern, simply remove the pattern sheet from the back of this book and trace it on to your fabric. You need to first put the fabric into your hoop and then place your hoop against the pattern making sure to centre the pattern in the middle of the hoop. You then need a flat surface to trace your pattern on to your fabric. You can use a table or a tracing board or simply hold it up against a window pane. I find this is the easiest and cheapest way to trace my design.

You then simply trace the pattern on to the back side of your hoop. You can then remove the fabric from the hoop, turn it around and put it back in the right side up. To transfer the pattern into the hoop, I recommend using a blue, water soluble marker. These markers can be found in most craft stores or online. Once your embroidery piece is complete, all you have to do is use cold water to wash away the markings.

Hoop stands aren't essential and they can be expensive so you don't need one. However, if you suffer from wrist pain they are a worthwhile investment.

MISCELLANEOUS

Before you get started there are few more things you might want to have handy. Firstly, **a pair of scissors**. They don't have to be anything fancy, as long as they are sharp enough to cut a strand of embroidery thread easily. However, if you make a mistake and need to cut out some stitches, tiny embroidery scissors will be your best friend. You can find specialist embroidery scissors in most craft stores, but the cutest ones are online. I find Etsy a great source of good embroidery supplies.

Secondly, you will need some **thread bobbins**. Small cardboard bobbins are all you need. They can be found in the embroidery section of your craft store. They are great to store your threads on and help you keep track of what colour code of thread you are using. They also mean your embroidery threads don't end up as one big, tangled mess.

Thirdly, and another dream tool for organisers, are **plastic storage containers** for your bobbins. Use them to help you keep track of what colour codes of threads you have on hand. Again, they can be found at most craft stores and online.

If like me, you have carpal tunnel syndrome and suffer from wrist pain, **a hoop stand** is a magical piece of equipment. A hoop stand saves your wrists from constantly having to hold onto your hoop while you're stitching. These can usually only be found online, and if you aren't a huge stitcher, definitely are not a necessity, but they are wonderful to have on hand if your wrists start hurting but you can't put your stitching down!

Lastly, **a cup of coffee**. Or tea. Because what is more relaxing than drinking a hot mug of your favourite beverage while enjoying the steady rhythm of stitching?

Now, let's get started. Get your pattern ready to trace, get comfortable and let's create our first design!

chapter two: stitch guide

Once you have your supplies, it's time to learn how to use them. This chapter focuses on all the embroidery stitches you will need to master in order to create the patterns in this book.

Embroidery stitches are, for the most part, really simple to understand and create. The most important thing to remember is to always tie a knot at the end of your thread before starting. If you don't, you risk pulling your thread all the way through the fabric and having stitches that are so loose that they bunch up and look lumpy. A good tip is to always tie a knot at the end of your strand of thread before you even thread your needle. It is also important to remember not to tie the two ends of your thread together after you have threaded your needle. Tie a knot, thread your needle, and leave the thread

loose like a tail. When you run out of thread, simply weave your needle into your stitches on the back of the hoop to secure your new piece of thread.

These are practice stitches and I recommend creating them on a seperate piece of fabric before jumping into the patterns in this book. Make them over and over again until you are comfortable with each stitch and then move on. I recommend using all six strands of your chosen thread and a large gauge needle when practicing these. That way, you can clearly see your stitches and can easily backtrack to see where you went wrong.

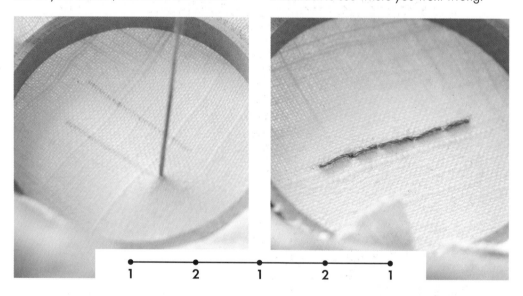

BASIC (STRAIGHT LINE) STITCH This stitch is simple and you'll use it a lot. Bring your needle up at **1** and back down into the fabric at **2**. Continue forward along the pattern as shown.

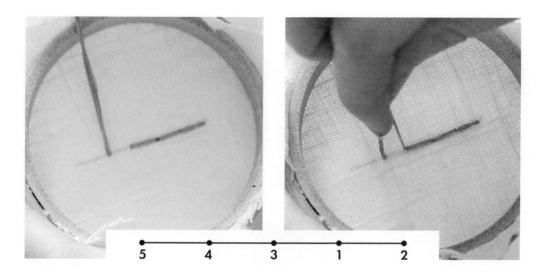

BACK STITCH This stitch will be used to outline and create flower stems. This is one of the most used stitches in embroidery, so make sure you master this one.

Start by bringing your needle up at **1**, and then pulling it down at **2**. Then come back up at **3** and down at **1**. Then up at **4** and back down at **3**. This is basically a backwards **BASIC STITCH**. Continue along the line as shown above.

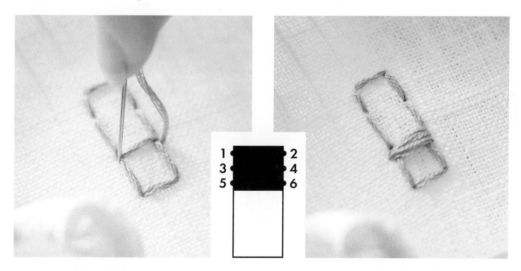

SATIN STITCH OUTLINED This stitch is used to fill in spaces, like the leaves and petals in my designs. This is another of the most used embroidery stitches so really study and practice it too. There are two ways to satin stitch. The first way is by filling in an outline. Usually the outline will be stitched first using **BACK STITCHES**. Then, you fill in the outline with satin stitch. Stay just outside the outline, bringing the needle up at **1** and down at **2**. Keep moving along, staying just outside the outline and keep your stitches tight and very close together as shown above.

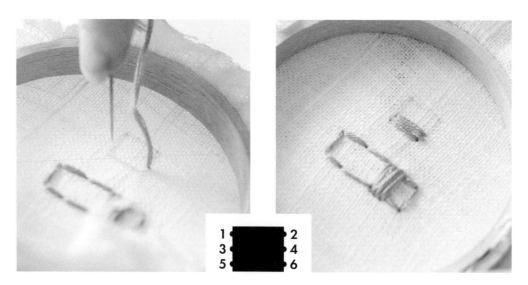

SATIN STITCH The second way to satin stitch is without using a pre-stitched outline. This creates a more organic and natural look. For this method, you will need to keep your stitches just touching an outline you have created with a pencil or marker. Keep your stitches tight and close together.

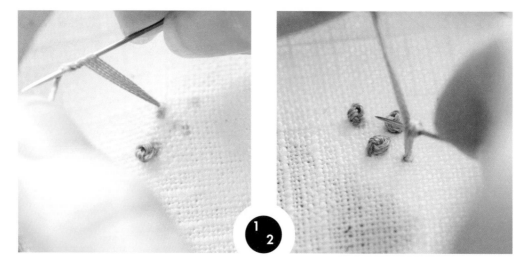

FRENCH KNOTS are used mostly for small detailing, and are probably the trickiest of stitches to master. Start this stitch by bringing your needle up at **1**. Then, holding the thread tight with the hand not holding the needle, wrap your thread around the needle and plunge the needle back down into the fabric slightly over at **2**. The most important thing is to keep the thread super tight, or the knot will look bunchy. In most French knots you will need to wrap the thread two to three times around the needle before putting the needle back through the fabric. However, sometimes it will be more than this, so in each pattern look out for my instructions for how many times you need to wrap the thread around the needle.

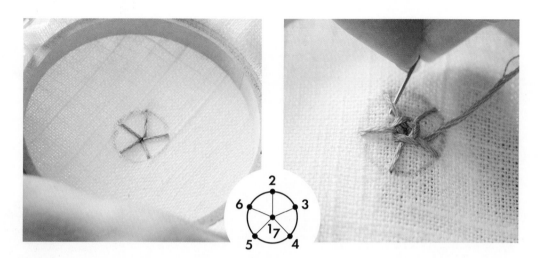

ROSE WHEEL STITCH (or WOVEN WHEEL STITCH) As the name suggests, this is the stitch you will use to create roses. Unlike the other stitches, the most important thing to remember here is to keep your thread loose. For these stitches, you will always use a full cut of thread, which means using all six strands. Start by bringing your needle up at **1**, then down at **2**. Then back up at **1**, and down at **3**. Up at **1**, down at **4**. Up at **1**, down at **5**. And up at **1** and down at **6**. This should create something that looks like the five spokes of a wheel. Once all five spokes are stitched, bring the needle up at **7** and start by weaving your needle in between the spokes. Over, under. Over, under. Keep the thread loose and, if you run out of thread, simply pull your needle through the fabric, rethread it, and bring it up in the same spot you ended. To finish, pull the needle down through the fabric and weave the tail through the back of the rose.

LAZY DAISY STITCH This stitch is used for petals and florals. These stitches can be a little tricky, so take your time with these. Just like the **ROSE WHEEL STITCH**, you will always use a full cut of all six strands. Thread your needle and bring your needle up at **1**. Then, slightly piercing it down at **2**, slip the needle forward just a tiny bit and bring the tip of the needle back up through the fabric at **3**. Then take the thread and loop it around the tip of the needle. Don't make these too tight. Put your needle back through the fabric at **4**, so you have created a small loop around the much larger one, anchoring it in place. You can then fill these in with thick **BASIC STITCHES**, but keep them just outside the petal.

chapter three: the basics

The patterns in this chapter will help you master the most basic embroidery stitches. Inspired by simple leaves, herbs and roses, these projects build on your skills so you are ready to tackle the more complex designs later in the book. Even if you have tried embroidery before, work through these patterns to reacquaint yourself with the basic stitches. Practice makes perfect!

simple leaves and stems

"And this our life, exempt from public haunt, finds tongues in trees, books in the running brooks, sermons in stones, and good in everything. I would not change it."

As You Like It, William Shakespeare

Materials:

- One 6" (15.2cm) embroidery hoop
- One 8"x8" (20.3 x 20.3cm) piece of white fabric, preferably linen
- One 5 gauge needle
- One 3 gauge needle
- DMC embroidery thread
  3347 medium yellow green
  3346 hunter green
  3348 light yellow green
- Blue water soluble marker
- Simple Leaves & Stems Pattern from the Patterns section of the book

Leaves are one of the most important features of my patterns as I find they give a coherence to the overall design. Leaves also make a great fillers linking floral designs together well. This project uses the easiest of stitches and is a great first pattern to start with.

I chose a quote from As You Like It to accompany this pattern. Duke Senior has been banished by his younger brother to the Forest of Ardenne with a group of his loyal men. Here, he is no longer haunted by having to keep up appearances at court and is learning to find beauty in the simpler things in life. Like Duke Senior, I believe in finding joy in the simple things and I think this project is a perfect example of this. There is also a real pleasure in the steady repetition of making these simple stitches. Don't be impatient to move on to the next project. There is plenty of time to learn the harder stitches you'll need to make the larger, more extravagant pieces later in this book.

INSTRUCTIONS

1. Start by inserting the fabric into the hoop. Linen doesn't have a right or wrong side so, unless you're using a patterned fabric, it doesn't matter which way up you insert the fabric in the hoop. Place the taut fabric against your chosen tracing surface (a window or table) and trace the pattern onto the fabric using a blue water soluble marker. You do not need to trace the lines inside the leaves onto the fabric; these are there merely as guidelines for the stitches you will make later in the pattern.

2. Start by outlining the leaves. You will need to split the medium yellow green thread (3347) into two groups of three strands. I also refer to this as a half-split cut throughout this book. Tie a knot at the end and then thread it into your 5 gauge needle.

3. Starting at the tip of one of the leaves, begin outlining using BACK STITCH. Complete all the leaves using this same stitch. If you run out of thread, continue by threading your needle with more medium yellow green (3347) and keep

stitching. Remember, after each cut of thread, tie off your thread tail so your stitches don't fall out.

4. Switching to the hunter green thread (3346), thread your 3 gauge needle with all six strands, and begin to stitch the stems between each leaf using BACK STITCH, until all your leaves are connected as shown.

5. Once you have completed the outlines and stems, you can fill the leaves in using the same medium yellow green thread (3347) in SATIN STITCH. I find it easiest to start from just outside the tip of the leaf, bringing my needle back down into the fabric just at the middle of the base of the leaf. Then I fan out my

stitches on either side. Remember to stay just outside of the outline you created. When you have finished the pattern, you shouldn't be able to see the BACK STITCH outline.

6. Finally, on to the detailing! This is one of the most important parts of any embroidery pattern, as it really makes the piece come to life. Tie a knot at the end of three strands of the light yellow green shade of thread (3348) and switch back to the 5 gauge needle. You will now use BASIC STITCH in the centre of all the leaves. Bring your needle up at the base of the leaf and down in the centre of the leaf, close to the tip. Continue to do this to on every leaf. Vary the length

of each stitch so the leaves aren't strictly uniform, just as they would be in nature. Then, using the same technique, detail some leaves using BASIC STITCH. Make sure some leaves have more light green stitches at the top, while others have light green stitches which start at the base and end in the centre of each leaf. The main thing to remember is that not every leaf has to be exactly the same and perfect.

7. Once your piece is complete, rinse the blue marks out with cold or lukewarm water and allow the fabric to dry before finishing the hoop. You can finish the hoop one of four ways: RING STITCH, LAYERING, QUICK CUT, or FOLD+GLUE, outlined in Chapter Six.

EXTRAS

■ You can always add cute little phrases like "Plant Lady" or "Plants for Life" to give extra detail to the piece.

■ Try hot gluing pom-pom Ric Rac around the edge of the hoop to jazz the piece up.

■ Instead of finishing the piece in the hoop, try stitching it to a pillow or an item of clothing.

■ Add a name and birth date and use the piece as a gift or birth announcement.

rosemary sprig arrangement

*"There's rosemary, that's for remembrance; pray,
love, remember; and there is pansies. that's for thoughts."*

Hamlet, William Shakespeare

Materials:

- One 6" (15.2cm) embroidery hoop

- One 8"x8" (20.3 x 20.3cm) piece of white fabric, preferably linen

- One 5 gauge needle

- One 3 gauge needle

- DMC embroidery thread

  937 medium avocado green

  936 very dark avocado green

  935 dark avocado green

  829 very dark golden olive

  3830 terracotta

- Blue water soluble marker

- Rosemary Sprig Arrangement Pattern from the Patterns section of the book

Using the leaves and stems from the last pattern, this pattern is created by adding in some sprigs of rosemary and red berries. When designing bouquet arrangements, I like to use sprays of berries because they link the flowers and leaves together perfectly.

I chose a Shakespeare quote from Hamlet for this design. In the play, poor mad Ophelia hands out bunches of flowers to those around her to express feelings she could not say out loud. She gives a sprig of rosemary to her brother, Laertes, as a silent way of telling him to "remember me". You won't go mad making this piece but the French knots might give you problems! They can be tricky, but if you make sure to take your time over them and be patient, they will turn out just fine.

INSTRUCTIONS

1. Start by inserting the fabric into the hoop. Linen doesn't have a right or wrong side so, unless you're using a patterned fabric, it doesn't matter which way up you insert the fabric in the hoop. Place the taut fabric against your chosen tracing surface (a window or table) and trace the pattern onto the fabric using a blue water soluble marker. You do not need to trace the lines inside the leaves onto the fabric; these are there merely as guidelines for the stitches you will make later in the pattern.

2. Start by outlining the leaves first. Cut a length of your very dark avocado green thread (936) and split in half, so that you have two groups of three threads. Thread your needle and using the BACK STITCH, outline some of the leaves.

3. Now splitting your medium avocado green thread (937) in half, use BACK STITCH and outline the rest of the leaves. It doesn't matter which leaves are which colour, that is totally up to you!

4. Fill the leaf outlines in with the same colour thread using SATIN STITCH. Stay just outside the outline for neat lines. If you run out of thread, tie off the tail, rethread your needle and continue where you left off.

5. Now, picking up a half split cut of very dark avocado green (936), create a single vein in the medium avocado green (937) leaves using a BASIC STITCH, starting at the base of the leaf. Do the same with the medium avocado green (937) strand and the very dark avocado green (936) leaves.

6. Take a piece of dark avocado (935), and split into two groups of three strands. Thread your needle, and

using BACK STITCH, connect the leaves with the stems.

7. Using very dark golden olive (829) BACK STITCH the rosemary and berry stems.

8. Once you have completed all the stems, cut a length of dark avocado thread (935), split it in half and thread your needle. Using BASIC STITCH, create small, downwards facing stitches beginning a few centimetres away from the stem and end back on the stem, covering the brown thread. Create these angled stitches up and down both sides of the stems to make the rosemary sprigs.

9. The final step is to create the red berries using the FRENCH KNOTs. Using all six strands of the terracotta thread (3830), create the FRENCH KNOTs by looping the thread twice around the needle, before plunging it back down into the fabric. Remember to keep your thread tight to avoid sloppy and inconsistent knots. Place the knots where you have marked the berry shapes with the blue marker pen. If you want to vary the texture, try layering a few knots on top of one another.

10. Once your piece is complete, rinse the blue marker pen out with lukewarm water and allow the fabric to dry before finishing the hoop. You can finish the hoop one of four ways: RING STITCH, LAYERING, QUICK CUT, or FOLD+GLUE - as outlined in Chapter Six.

EXTRAS
- Try hot gluing pom-pom Ric Rac around the edge of the hoop to jazz the piece up.
- This project would be adorable as a patch to embellish your favourite jacket. Simply cut out the stitching, fuse to iron-on adhesive and then attach to your chosen item of clothing.
- Stitch "Rosemary for Remembrance" in the hoop and hang it in your kitchen!

winter roses

*"What's in a name? That which we call a rose
By any other name would smell as sweet."*

Romeo and Juliet, William Shakespeare

Materials:

- One 6'' (15.2cm) embroidery hoop

- One 8''x8'' (20.3 x 20.3cm) piece of white fabric, preferably linen

- One 5 gauge needle

- One 3 gauge needle

- DMC embroidery thread

  840 medium beige brown

  3051 dark green grey

  3052 medium green grey

  3865 winter white

  645 very dark beaver grey

  3781 dark mocha brown

- Blue water soluble marker

- Winter Roses Pattern from the Patterns section of the book

In this pattern, you will learn to stitch the ROSE WHEEL STITCH to create the roses, which are my absolutely favourite flower to stitch. The most important thing to remember with this project, is to take your time. If you rush making your roses, they can look messy and loopy. Take your time and weave your needle carefully between the spokes.

For this romantic winter bouquet, I needed a beautiful Shakespeare quote as inspiration. And is there anything quite as romantic as this famous quote from Romeo and Juliet?

INSTRUCTIONS

1. Start by inserting the fabric into the hoop. Linen doesn't have a right or wrong side so, unless you're using a patterned fabric, it doesn't matter which way up you insert the fabric in the hoop. Place the taut fabric against your chosen tracing surface (a window or table) and trace the pattern onto the fabric using a blue water soluble marker. My advice is to trace the roses and leaves first, and the details afterwards.

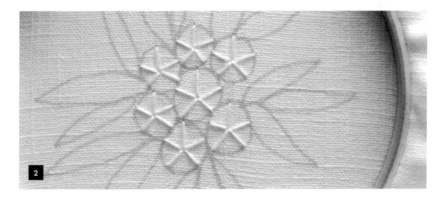

2. Start by taking a long cut of the winter white thread (3865). Using all six strands, thread a 3 gauge needle and tie a knot at the end. Using the ROSE WHEEL STITCH from the stitch guide, start by stitching all the 'spokes' for each of the seven roses.

3. Next, fill in the roses with more winter white thread (3865). Remember, if your thread ends before your rose is complete, simply re-thread your needle, and start where you ran out. The most important thing is not to pull your thread too tight as you weave between the spokes. Make sure any tails left on the backside of the stitching are woven into the back stitches and snipped off, so you don't accidentally pull on them and make the roses loopy.

4. Splitting your dark green grey thread (3051) in half into two three strand pieces, thread a 5 gauge needle and outline half of the leaves using BACK STITCH. Then with the medium green grey thread (3052), do the same with the other half of the leaves. It's not

important which leaves are which shade of green, as long as half are one shade and half the other.

5. Fill in the leaves with the same colours, using SATIN STITCH. Remember, always stay just outside the outline for a neat look.

6. You will then move on to the Scabiosa pods. These are probably some of my favourite flowers to stitch. They are beautiful decorative fillers. Start with all six strands of medium beige brown thread (840) and stitch large FRENCH KNOTs by looping the thread around the 3 gauge needle three or four times. Fill in all the empty space between the roses.

7. Next, splitting a long piece of very dark beaver grey thread (645) in half, stitch smaller FRENCH KNOTs inside the light brown ones. Loop the thread around your needle once or twice for these. You want the grey knots smaller than the brown ones but still to show up well.

8. Now take a long piece of dark mocha brown thread (3781) and thread a 5 gauge needle with three strands. With long BASIC STITCHes, create the bare stems between the leaves.

9. Lastly, for the vein details (see main picture) use the opposite shade of green to the leaves and stitch one, long BASIC STITCH, ending it close to the leaf tip.

10. Rinse the blue marker pen out and allow the fabric to dry. You can finish the hoop one of four ways: RING STITCH, LAYERING, QUICK CUT, or FOLD+GLUE, as outlined in Chapter Six.

EXTRAS
- Hot glue glittery white pom-poms around the edge of the hoop to add a winter feel to the piece.
- Add the word "Christmas" and the year underneath the bouquet for a Christmas decoration. Centre the bouquet higher in the hoop to make room for the words
- Instead of finishing the piece in the hoop, try stitching it to a pillow or article of clothing.

chapter four: detailed

The four floral embroidery patterns in this chapter have all been designed to help you build on the skills you learned in the previous chapter. You will be using all the same embroidery stitches you have worked with before, but in different ways. You will be working on combining your stitches to create more complex and detailed floral designs.

spring floral arrangement

*"From you have I been absent in the spring, When proud-pied April,
dress'd in all his trim, Hath put a spirit of youth in everything."*

Sonnet 98, William Shakespeare

Materials:

- One 6" (15.2cm) inch embroidery hoop

- One 8"x8" (20.3 x 20.3cm) piece of white fabric, preferably linen

- One 5 gauge needle

- One 3 gauge needle

- DMC embroidery thread

  3865 winter white

  3713 very light salmon

  153 lilac

  725 topaz

  422 light hazelnut brown

  731 dark olive green

  733 medium olive green

- Blue water soluble marker

- Spring Floral Arrangement With Room for Words Pattern from the Patterns section of the book

Inspired by Shakespeare's springtime sonnet, this brings together all the stitches you have learned so far in a pretty spring design. As a complete contrast to the winter tones of the previous project, I wanted to use a springtime pallet of colours that reminded me of my pink childhood bedroom with its purple flower fairy wallpaper.

I also created this design to make it easy for you to add a quote to give it your own twist. I believe it is very important as an artist to look for ways to add individuality to your work, so use the space around the floral design to add words that are meaningful to you.

INSTRUCTIONS

1. Start by inserting the fabric into the hoop. Linen doesn't have a right or wrong side so, unless you're using a patterned fabric, it doesn't matter which way up you insert the fabric in the hoop. Place the taut fabric against your chosen tracing surface (a window or table) and trace the pattern onto the fabric using a blue water soluble marker. My advice is to trace the roses, leaves and hanging lilacs first. Then trace the other details afterwards.

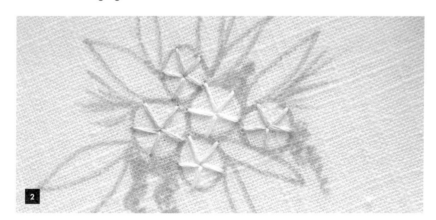

2. Now starting with a long piece of winter white thread (3865), use all 6 strands and stitch the spokes for the two white roses using a 3 gauge needle. Then do the same with very light salmon thread (3713) to make the other roses.

3. Using the same colours and all 6 strands of the thread, fill in the roses using the ROSE WHEEL STITCH. Remember, take your time and don't pull the thread too tight. Once your roses are filled in, take the opposite colour and stitch a few small FRENCH KNOTs in the centre of the roses. You don't want these to be too big, so only loop your thread once or twice around the needle. Be very careful not to pull too much on your rose stitches.

4. Taking a long piece of dark olive green thread (731), split it in half and, using a 5 gauge needle, outline all the leaves using BACK STITCH. At this stage, check that your fabric is still tight in your hoop

to avoid your stitching going bunchy. Tighten your hoop if you find your fabric is losing its tension.

5. Still using the other half of the piece of dark olive green thread (731), fill in the leaves using SATIN STITCH. Remember, stitch just outside the outline when filling the leaves in to ensure a neat edge. Use your fingers to pull the thread to keep the stitches even.

6. Now, move on to stitching the lilacs. Using half a piece of lilac thread (153), fill in the pattern with small FRENCH KNOTs. These knots need to be small, so loop the thread around your needle two or three times.

7. Taking half a strand of medium olive green thread (733), stitch the vein details in the leaves using long BASIC STITCHes. Start at the base and end at the top of each leaf. Next, using the same thread, stitch the stems of the billy balls using small BACK STITCHes.

8. Using a whole piece of topaz thread (725), stitch a single FRENCH KNOT for each billy ball. These need to be really big knots, so loop the thread around the 3 gauge needle at least four to five times.

9. Lastly, split the light hazelnut brown thread (422) in half and stitch the wheat stems by making single BASIC STITCHes in varying lengths.

10. Once your piece is complete, rinse the blue marker pen out with lukewarm water and dry the fabric before finishing the hoop. You can finish the hoop in several different ways: RING STITCH, LAYERING, QUICK CUT, or FOLD+GLUE, as outlined in detail in Chapter Six.

EXTRAS

■ The easiest way to add a quote is to use three strand BACK STITCHes.

■ Add some cute Ric Rac to the edges of the hoop to dress up the piece.

autumnal bouquet

*"That time of year thou mayst in me behold, When yellow leaves,
or none, or few, do hang, Upon those boughs which shake against
the cold, Bare ruin'd choirs where late the sweet birds sang.."*

Sonnet 73, William Shakespeare

Materials:

- One 6'' (15.2cm) embroidery hoop
- One 8''x8'' (20.3 x 20.3cm) piece of white fabric, preferably linen
- One 5 gauge needle
- DMC embroidery thread

  3781 mocha brown

  3820 dark straw

  472 ultra light avocado green

  471 very light avocado green

  319 very dark pistachio green

  160 medium petrol blue

  161 dark petrol blue

  841 light beige brown

  3713 very light salmon

  224 very light shell pink
- Blue water soluble marker
- Autumnal Bouquet Pattern from the Patterns section of the book

This pattern will be your first experience using a non-outlined version of satin stitch. I have always liked this method more than other methods, as it creates a more organic feel to your stitches. It is essential that you make sure your stitches stay right on the outline you make with your marker.

Autumn will always be my favourite season. I love the crisp morning air, the leaves turning shades of gold and red, and the apples that swell on the branches of the tree behind my house. My sister, Emma, always plants sunflower seeds in the spring and by autumn the flowers are as big as my head. My Grandma who loved flowers would have been so proud of my sister's sunflowers and this design is dedicated to them both.

INSTRUCTIONS

1. Start by inserting the fabric into the hoop. Linen doesn't have a right or wrong side so, unless you're using a patterned fabric, it doesn't matter which way up you insert the fabric in the hoop. Place the taut fabric against your chosen tracing surface (a window or table) and trace the pattern onto the fabric using a blue water soluble marker. My advice is to trace the sunflowers, leaves and stems first. You can either trace the rest of the pattern at the same time or wait and trace them when you come to them in the pattern.

2. Start by splitting a long piece of mocha brown thread (3781) in half and begin stitching the FRENCH KNOTs for the sunflower centres. These should be stitched tightly together using small knots, so only wrap your thread around your needle once or twice.

3. Once the centres are done, split a piece of dark straw thread (3820) in half and stitch the sunflower petals using SATIN STITCH without an outline. Stitching them like this gives the petals a more organic, natural feel. Start your SATIN STITCHes by bringing the needle up at the tip of each petal, and then down at the base of the centre. Work the stitches out from that centre stitch, stitching right up to the marker outline. Keep your stitches tight, so the fabric doesn't get bunched underneath.

4. After you have completed the sunflowers, take a full strand of very light avocado green thread (471) and stitch the leaf stems by making small BACK STITCHes (See illustration 5).

5. Stitch the leaves in the same way as the petals, using smooth SATIN STITCHes. Take a long piece of ultra light avocado green thread (472), split it in half and start stitching at the tip of each leaf. Take care to keep your stitches on the marker lines and angle them downwards towards the stems.

6. Take a strand of very light avocado green thread (471), split it in half and stitch the leaf veins. Start at the base of each leaf and finish them higher up, using simple BASIC STITCHes.

7. Using light beige brown thread (841) for the leafless stems, very dark pistachio green thread (319) for the fern stems, and mocha brown thread (3781) for the berry stems, stitch the stems in BACK STITCH using three strands of thread.

8. Stitch the berries in FRENCH KNOT stitches using six strands of medium petrol blue (160) and dark petrol blue (161) thread, looping the thread around the needle once or twice.

9. Take three strands of the pistachio green thread (319) and stitch the needles on the fern stems. Create these by making small BASIC STITCHes in small groups down the stem. Angle the stitches down and overlap them across the stem.

10. Finally, take a piece of very light shell pink thread (224) and a piece of very light salmon thread (3713) and split both in half. Stitch the hanging amaranthus using the FRENCH KNOT stitch, alternating between the two shades of pink. Keep these stitches small and tight by looping the thread around your needle two or three times.

11. Once your piece is complete, rinse the blue marker pen out using cold to lukewarm water. Allow the fabric to dry before finishing the hoop. You can finish the hoop in several different ways: RING STITCH, LAYERING, QUICK CUT, or FOLD+GLUE, as outlined in detail in Chapter Six.

sherbet bouquet

"Shall I compare thee to a summer's day? Thou art more lovely and more temperate. Rough winds do shake the darling buds of May, And summer's lease hath all too short a date."

Sonnet 18, William Shakespeare

Materials:
- One 6'' (15.2cm) embroidery hoop
- One 8''x8'' (20.3 x 20.3cm) piece of white fabric, preferably linen
- One 5 gauge needle
- One 3 gauge needle
- DMC embroidery thread

  3865 winter white

  3771 dark peach

  3689 light mauve

  353 light peach

  3362 dark pine green

  3363 medium pine green

  3364 pine green

  3855 light autumn gold

  223 light shell pink
- Blue water soluble marker
- Sherbet Bouquet Pattern from the Patterns section of the book

When I was little, and my family would make trips to my Oma's house during the summer, she always had a tub of frozen sherbet in the freezer. Peach, orange and strawberry flavours, all mixed together in swirls. When I sat down to create this pattern, I wanted to capture that memory whilst teaching you the final stitch you need to learn to make the rest of the patterns in this book.

I think Shakespeare always wrote such beautiful descriptions of the changing seasons, because in England they seem to slip so gently into each other. In America, where I live, the seasons change so dramatically they seem to slam into each other. I wanted to capture that gentle slide from spring to summer in this bouquet arrangement design.

INSTRUCTIONS

1 Start by inserting the fabric into the hoop. Linen doesn't have a right or wrong side so, unless you're using a patterned fabric, it doesn't matter which way up you insert the fabric in the hoop. Place the taut fabric against your chosen tracing surface (a window or table) and trace the pattern onto the fabric using a blue water soluble marker. My advice is to trace the roses, peonies, hanging amaranthus and leaves first. Then trace the other details on afterwards.

2. Start with the peach peonies. This will be your first time using the LAZY DAISY STITCH. Start by cutting a long six strand piece of light peach thread (353). Using a 3 gauge needle, outline the petals of the peonies using the LAZY DAISY STITCH and then fill in the petals with thick, simple BASIC STITCHes keeping just outside the outline, until the petals are complete.

3. Make spokes using the ROSE WHEEL STITCH, six strands of winter white (3865), light shell pink (223) and light mauve (3689) thread and a 3 gauge needle.

4. Stitch the roses using the same colours and the ROSE WHEEL STITCH and six strands of thread. Keep the stitches loose so the roses don't go lumpy. If there

are spaces between your roses simply fill these in with larger FRENCH KNOTs in the same colour.

5. Using FRENCH KNOTs stitch the hanging amaranthus with three strands of light autumn gold thread (3855), keeping each knot tight and close to the others and looping the thread around the 5 gauge needle once or twice.

6. Split a strand of dark pine green thread (3362) in half and using BACK STITCH, make the berry stems.

7. After the stems, make the berries on the tips of the stems with large FRENCH KNOTS. Use six strands of dark peach thread (3771), wrapped three times around a 3 gauge needle.

8. Now, stitch the leaves using a three gauge needle, all three shades of green thread - dark pine green (3362), medium pine green (3363) and pine green (3364) and SATIN STITCH. These leaves will not be outlined to create an organic look to them. Alternate the shades of green evenly making sure you don't have two leaves of the same colour next to each other. Remember to keep your stitches on the pencil or marker outline. Place your first stitch in the centre of the leaf and starting at the tip, end at the base. Then work outwards from the centre to fill in the whole leaf.

9. Your next step is to add the detailing of the veins to each leaf. For dark pine green (3362) leaves, use medium pine green (3363) for the veins. For medium pine green (3363) leaves, use the pine green (3364) for the veins. For the pine green (3364) leaves, use the dark pine green (3362) for the veins. Create the veins with a BASIC STITCH starting at the base of each leaf and ending higher up in the centre.

10. Lastly, create the stems for the leaves, using a three strand piece of dark pine green thread (3362). Use BACK STITCH, creating small stitches to connect the leaves.

11. Once your piece is complete, rinse the blue marker pen out with cold to lukewarm water and allow the fabric to dry before finishing the hoop. You can finish the hoop in one of four ways: RING STITCH, LAYERING, QUICK CUT, or FOLD+GLUE, as outlined in Chapter Six.

gem tone bouquet

"She is mine own, And I as rich in having such a jewel, As twenty seas, of all their sand were pearl, The water nectar, and the rocks pure gold."

The Two Gentlemen of Verona, William Shakespeare

Materials:

- One 6'' (15.2cm) embroidery hoop

- One 8''x8'' (20.3 x 20.3cm) piece of white fabric, preferably linen

- One 5 gauge needle

- One 3 gauge needle

- DMC embroidery thread

  400 dark mahogany

  3363 medium pine green

  3364 pine green

  869 very dark hazelnut brown

  3865 winter white

  310 black

  3815 dark celadon green

  680 dark old gold

  3771 dark peach

  3803 dark mauve

  3778 light terracotta

  3813 light blue green

- Blue water soluble marker

- Gem Tone Bouquet Pattern from the Patterns section of the book

For this piece, I had chosen the colours before I even started the design! I knew I wanted rich gem tones, inspired by the colours of Princess Eugenie's wedding. Even though I am an American, I hold tightly to my European roots, and often find myself spellbound by the wonder of the British royal family. I wanted this piece to feel regal and this wonderful Shakespearian quote inspired my design.

INSTRUCTIONS

1. Start by inserting the fabric into the hoop. Linen doesn't have a right or wrong side so, unless you're using a patterned fabric, it doesn't matter which way up you insert the fabric in the hoop. Place the taut fabric against your chosen tracing surface (a window or table) and trace the pattern onto the fabric using a blue water soluble marker. My advice is to trace the roses, anemones, peonies, and leaves first. Then trace the details on afterwards.

2. Take a six strand piece of dark peach thread (3771) and using a three gauge needle, start with the peony bunches. Use the LAZY DAISY STITCH to create the outline of the flowers. Then fill them in with the same colour. Keep these filler stitches thick and just outside the marker outline.

51

3. Next, taking a six strand piece of dark mauve thread (3803), stitch the five wheel spokes of the ROSE WHEEL STITCHes. Remember to keep these tight and always pull your needle through at the same place in the centre.

4. Now, using the same colour, weave your needle in and out of the spokes, keeping the thread loose enough so you don't create bunches or loops in your roses. Be careful not to catch your needle in the peonies and pull these stitches out.

5. Once you have completed all the roses, take a piece of black thread (310) and split it in half. Thread a 5 gauge needle, and create the black centres of

the anemone flowers using FRENCH KNOT stitches. Make sure to keep these stitches small and close together, using only one or two loops around the needle.

6. To create the petals of the anemones, take a piece of winter white thread (3865) and split it in half. Using small BACK STITCHes, outline the petals. Then fill them in using the same colour and the outlined version of SATIN STITCH. Keep these stitches tight and close together. You can smooth the stitches out with your finger as you go along to keep your stitching neat. Once you have filled in the petals, take three strands of black thread (310) and create the tiny FRENCH KNOTs inside some of the petals.

7. Moving on to the leaves, take three strands of the medium pine green (3363) and pine green (3364) threads and stitch the leaves with the SATIN STITCH. These do not need to be outlined first, so your leaves have a natural organic look. It is not important which leaves are stitched in the medium pine green (3363) and which are in the pine green (3364). The more random the placement of the colours, the more natural and organic the look of your finished piece.

8. To create the stems and veins of the leaves, take three strands of very dark hazelnut brown thread (869), thread your needle and stitch them using BASIC STITCH.

9. Moving on to the billy balls, take three strands of dark old gold thread (680) and using the FRENCH KNOT stitch, create these flowers. Make sure to keep your knots tight and close together, looping the thread around the needle two or three times.

10. Now, take three strands of medium pine green thread (3363), and stitch all the green stems using the BACK STITCH.

11. For the inner blue-green berries, take three strands of dark celadon green thread (3815) and create using FRENCH KNOT stitches. Make sure to keep these stitches small and close together by looping your thread around the needle twice.

12. For the pink spiky flowers, take three strands of light terracotta thread (3778) and stitch them using small diagonal BASIC STITCHes, overlapping the stem.

13. The penultimate stitches are the tiny FRENCH KNOTs made using dark celadon green thread (3813) on the outer blue-berry stems. Create these by using a three thread strand of thread, wrapping your thread around the needle twice.

14. The final addition to this design are the rusty orange hanging amaranthus. To create them, take three strands of dark mahogany thread (400), thread a 5 gauge needle, and stitch small FRENCH KNOTS

down the stems. Wrap your thread around the needle two or three times and keep the knots tight and full.

15. Once your piece is complete, rinse the blue marker pen out with cold or lukewarm water and allow the fabric to dry before finishing the hoop. You can finish the hoop in one of four ways RING STITCH, LAYERING, QUICK CUT, or FOLD+GLUE, as outlined in Chapter Six.

chapter five: intricate

The last three patterns in this book focus on bringing together all the aspects of design, colour choice and stitching you have learned so for to create more intricate floral designs. All the stitches you have mastered are combined in new and more complex ways. I can't wait for you to get started!

spring blooms bouquet

"Now, my fair'st friend, I would I had some flowers o' the spring that might become your time of day."

The Winter's Tale, William Shakespeare

Materials:

- One 6'' (15.2cm) embroidery hoop
- One 8''x8'' (20.3 x 20.3cm) piece of white linen
- One 5 gauge needle
- One 3 gauge needle
- DMC embroidery thread

  727 very light topaz

  3770 very light tawny

  402 very light mahogany

  869 very dark hazelnut brown

  3325 light baby blue

  3362 dark pine green

  3363 medium pine green

  3364 pine green

  3865 winter white

  502 blue green

  351 coral

  352 light coral

  353 peach

  3771 dark peach

  3829 very dark old gold

- Blue water soluble marker
- Spring Blooms Pattern from the Patterns Section of the book

Growing up, my front yard was full of enormous pink peony bushes. The big blousey flowers ranged from the palest pink to the most vibrant fuchsia. I wanted to capture the essence of those incredible peonies in this bouquet and create something a bride might carry down the aisle at her sunny May or June wedding.

I stitched this piece during one of the snowiest months of the year and this Shakespeare quote from the Winter's Tale reminded me that even in the deepest of winters, spring is always just around the corner.

INSTRUCTIONS

1. Start by inserting the fabric into the hoop. Linen doesn't have a right or wrong side so, unless you're using a patterned fabric, it doesn't matter which way up you insert the fabric in the hoop. Place the taut fabric against your chosen tracing surface (a window or table) and trace the pattern onto the fabric using a blue water soluble marker. My advice is to trace the large pink flowers, the peony, roses and larger leaves first. Then trace the smaller leaves, bluebells and other details on afterwards.

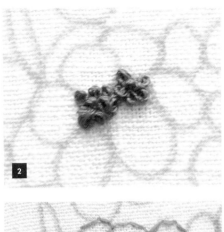

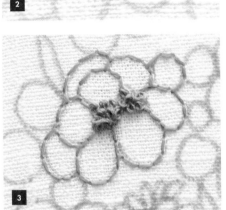

2. Begin your stitching by taking three strands of very dark old gold thread (3829). Create small FRENCH KNOTs in the centre of the large pink flowers. Wrap your thread once or twice around a 5 gauge needle to keep them small and close together. There should be no gaps where you can see the fabric.

3. Next, take a long strand of coral thread (351) and split it in half. Thread a 5 gauge needle and begin stitching around the outline of the pink flower with BACK STITCH. Do this one petal at a time rather than in one continuous outline so you don't lose where you are in the design. When you move on to the next petal, make sure your stitches touch the stitches of the previous petal .

4. Once you have outlined the pink flower, take a three strand piece of the same colour and fill in the petals using SATIN STITCH. Keep these stitches tight and close together; there should be no gaps between the long stitches. You might need to go back over your stitching and fill in the gaps which is very simple to do. Stitch one at a time, starting at the centre of each petal and working out from the centre to each side. Once the entire pink flower is filled in, you should still see a bit of definition between each petal because they were stitched one at a time. Now take three strands of light coral thread (352) and add in the lighter BASIC STITCHes. These can be randomly placed, but should be stitched out from the centre of the very dark old gold thread (3829) FRENCH KNOTs.

5. Next, move onto the pale pink peony. Taking a full strand of very light tawny thread (3770), use LAZY DAISY stitch to outline and fill in the large petals, using a 3 gauge needle.

6. Once the petals are all filled in, take three strands of dark peach thread (3771) and using a 5 gauge needle, stitch the BASIC STITCH details.

7. Now take full strands of winter white (3865) and peach (353) thread and using a 3 gauge needle, stitch the five spokes for each rose. Try your best to follow the pattern of colours I used in the illustratration.

8. Then using the same colours, weave in the roses using ROSE WHEEL STITCH. Remember, keep these stitches loose enough so they aren't loopy. If there are any odd spaces between roses - which is very common - fill them in with some contrasting coloured FRENCH KNOTS.

9. Next, take three strands of very light topaz thread (727) and stitch the yellow billy balls, using small

FRENCH KNOTs. Wrap your thread around a 5 gauge needle two or three times to keep the knots tight and close together.

10. Moving on to the orange amaranthus, take three strands of very light mahogany thread (402) and stitch small FRENCH KNOTs. Wrap your thread once or twice around the needle. You can keep these stitches a little bit looser to create a more natural look.

11. At this stage, you will notice a lot of space between the flowers. Take three strands of dark pine green thread (3362) and keeping the stitches close together fill in the space with outlined SATIN STITCH. Think of this stage as colouring inside the lines.

12. Now, take three strands of blue green thread (502) and stitch the five larger leaves using the non-

outlined SATIN STITCH. Start your stitching in the centre of the leaf outline and work out from there.

13. Stitch the leaf stems by using three strands of very dark hazelnut brown thread (869), using BASIC STITCH to connect the leaves to the bouquet body. Start in the leaf middle and end in the body of the bouquet.

14. Stitch the bluebell stems, using three strands of pine green thread (3364) to create medium sized BACK STITCHes following along the outline.

15. Create the bluebells with a full strand of light baby blue thread (3325) and a 3 gauge needle, making the outlines with LAZY DAISY STITCHes. Ensure the bottoms are as close to the stems as possible so they look connected to the stem. Then with the same colour,

fill in the bluebell petals.

16. Now stitch the smaller leaves in non-outlined SATIN STITCH using three strands of dark pine green (3362), medium pine green (3363) and pine green (3364) thread. Use the greens in a random way to create a natural look.

17. Connect all the leaves together and attach to the bouquet body by making small BACK STITCHes with three strands of dark pine green thread (3362).

18. Once your piece is complete, rinse the blue marker pen out with lukewarm water and allow the fabric to dry before finishing the hoop. You can finish the hoop in one of four ways: RING STITCH, LAYERING, QUICK CUT, or FOLD+GLUE, as outlined in Chapter Six.

midsummer bouquet

"I know a bank where the wild thyme blows, Where oxlips and the nodding violet grows, Quite over-canopied with luscious woodbine, With sweet musk-roses and with eglantine: There sleeps Titania sometime of the night, Lull'd in these flowers with dances and delight;"

A Midsummer Night's Dream, William Shakespeare

Materials:
- One 6 (15.2cm)embroidery hoop
- One 8''x8'' (20.3 x 20.3cm) piece of white fabric, preferably linen
- One 5 gauge needle
- One 3 gauge needle
- DMC embroidery thread

  3774 very light desert sand

  3779 ultra very light terracotta

  413 dark pewter gray

  414 dark steel gray

  3865 winter white

  3828 hazelnut brown

  680 dark old gold

  3363 medium pine green

  3364 pine green

  3772 very dark desert sand

  3770 very light tawny

  829 very dark golden olive

  3768 dark gray green
- Blue water soluble marker
- Midsummer Bouquet Pattern from the Patterns section of the book

For this design in the book, I wanted to choose a passage of Shakespeare that felt the most special to me. A Midsummer Night's Dream is one of Shakespeare's most popular comedy plays. Set in an enchanted forest with fairies, sparring lovers and a group of amateur actors putting on a play, A Midsummer Night's Dream was one of the first Shakespeare plays I read and the first of his plays I directed myself. These poetic lines are some of my favourite in all his works. There is something truly magical about this play, the lines and the characters. There has also been something truly magical about working on this book.

INSTRUCTIONS

1. Start by inserting the fabric into the hoop. Linen doesn't have a right or wrong side so, unless you're using a patterned fabric, it doesn't matter which way up you insert the fabric in the hoop. Place the taut fabric against your chosen tracing surface (a window or table) and trace the pattern onto the fabric using a blue water soluble marker. My advice is to trace the roses and leaves first. Then trace the other details on afterwards.

2. To begin stitching, take one strand of ultra very light terracotta thread (3779) Threading a 3 gauge needle with all six strands of the thread, create your ROSE WHEEL SPOKES for the three roses as shown.

65

3. Now, using six strands of the same colour thread, weave your needle in and out between the spokes, to create the roses. Remember to keep your thread tight enough in the spokes so that it does not appear loopy and tangled, but loose enough for the threads to spread out and create the roses.

4. In the same fashion, stitch the spokes for the other two roses in very light desert sand (3774) and very light tawny (3770) thread. Using the same needle and six strands of the same colour, fill in your roses. The key with stitching roses, is take your time and pay attention when you are going over and under the spokes.

5. The next step is to stitch the billy-balls. Taking a piece of hazelnut brown thread (3828), thread a three gauge needle with all 6 strands and fill in the circles

with FRENCH KNOTs. Use a double loop on these. Once you have completely filled in the circles, go back with three strands of dark old gold thread (680) and a 5 gauge needle, scattering a few single loop FRENCH KNOTs throughout for contrast and texture.

6. Moving on to the daisy bunches, take a piece of winter white thread (3865) and thread a three gauge needle with all 6 strands. Create the outline of the petals with LAZY DAISY STITCH and then go back and fill them in with just a few BASIC STITCHes.

7. Once your daisy bunches are complete, take a long strand of medium pine green thread (3363) and split in half. With a five gauge needle, use BACK STITCH to outline all the large, outside leaves.

8. Using three strands of the same colour, fill in the

leaves using SATIN STITCH. Try to keep these tight and remain as close to outline as possible.

9. To create detailing on these leaves, take a three strand of pine green thread (3364) and create BASIC STITCHes starting at the base of the leaves, and ending just before the tip. Then, using a few, smaller angled BASIC STITCHes, create the smaller veins.

10. Now for the thistles! These are incredibly simple and super fun to make! Cut the dark steel gray thread (414) and split in half. Then, with a 5 gauge needle fill the thistle in with small, delicate FRENCH KNOTs. You can either single or double loop them. Doing a mix of the two will also create some nice texture. Once you have filled them in, go back over with a few FRENCH KNOTs, using three strands of the dark pewter gray thread (413).

11. Keeping your 5 gauge needle threaded with three strands of the same colour, use BASIC STITCH to make a few needles coming up from the thistle body. Do the same with the dark steel gray thread (414).

12. The final step for the thistles are the stems. Take three strands of dark pewter gray thread (413), and create the stems with BACK STITCH.

13. Next, thread your 5 gauge needle with three strands of very dark desert sand thread (3772). Starting at the base of the dark pink amaranthus, create small FRENCH KNOTs by looping your thread twice around your needle before plunging your needle back down into the fabric. Remember, always keep the thread tight!

14. Take three strands of medium pine green thread

(3363) in half and thread your 5 gauge needle. In this step, it is really important to tie a knot at the end of the thread so the long stitches stay in place. To stitch the needles, simply follow the pattern lines with BASIC STITCHes, until you have filled the space.

15. Now is it time to create all the stems. Starting with the stems for the blue berries and red buds, take three strands of very dark golden olive thread (829) and stitch the stems using BACK STITCH. Then, with the same technique and three strands of pine green thread (3364), stitch the green stems.

16. For the little green leaves sprouting from the pine green stems, use the same amount of thread as the stems and stitch the leaves with non-outlined SATIN STITCHes. Keep your stitches right on your pencil or marker outline to ensure it looks neat and consistent.

17. Now for the blue berries, take three strands of dark gray green thread (3768) and create FRENCH KNOTs along the green and brown stems, looping the thread around your needle twice. The smaller the knots, the better.

18. Finally, take three strands of very dark desert sand thread (3722) and stitch the red buds. Using a 5 gauge needle, wrap the thread around it once when making them. Stack them neatly together to create the buds.

19. Once your piece is complete, rinse the blue marker pen out with cold to lukewarm water and allow the fabric to dry before finishing the hoop. You can finish the hoop in one of four ways: RING STITCH, LAYERING, QUICK CUT, or FOLD+GLUE, as outlined in Chapter Six.

spooky bouquet

"Double, double toil and trouble; Fire burn and cauldron bubble."

Macbeth, William Shakespeare

Materials:

- One 6'' (15.2cm) embroidery hoop
- One 8''x8'' (20.3 x 20.3cm) piece of white linen
- One 5 gauge needle
- One 3 gauge needle
- DMC embroidery thread

    310 black

    3770 very light tawny

    976 medium golden brown

    921 copper

    932 light antique blue

    151 pink

    731 dark olive green

    730 very dark olive green

    732 olive green

    733 medium olive green

    869 very dark hazelnut brown

    3834 medium grape

    783 medium topaz

    224 very light shell pink

    3859 light rosewood

- Blue water soluble marker
- Spooky Bouquet Pattern from the Patterns section of the book

On my first trip to England I spent a week at my friend Kyle's cottage. Her garden was full of colourful life. Dahlias of all sizes and colours bloomed right outside the cottage windows and I loved their sharp structured forms so much I knew immediately, I had to stitch them. I have always adored the Halloween colour combination of orange, purple, black and bright green, so I wanted to create a design that could incorporate those colours as well as dahlias. Maybe it's because of my Scottish heritage or maybe because I have a soft spot in my heart for Lady Macbeth, but Macbeth is one of my favourites of the great bard's plays and this quote is just so perfect for Halloween.

INSTRUCTIONS

1. Start by inserting the fabric into the hoop. Linen doesn't have a right or wrong side so, unless you're using a patterned fabric, it doesn't matter which way up you insert the fabric in the hoop. Place the taut fabric against your chosen tracing surface (a window or table) and trace the pattern onto the fabric using a blue water soluble marker. My advice is to trace the dahlias, anemones, roses and leaves first. Then trace the other details on afterwards.

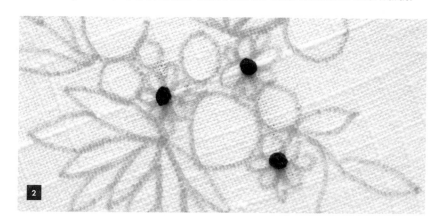

2. Start your stitching by creating the centres for the muted pink anemones. Take three strands of black thread (310) and make small FRENCH KNOTs. Wrap your thread around the 5 gauge needle once or twice to keep them tight and close together.

3. Create the anemone petals with six strands of very light tawny thread (3770). Use LAZY DAISY STITCH and a 3 gauge needle to create the outlines and then fill in the petals. Once you have stitched your anemones, add very tiny black (310) FRENCH KNOTs near the centre of the flowers, wrapping the thread around the 5 gauge needle once or twice. Keep them small and tight.

4. Moving on to the purple roses, take a full strand of dark grape thread (3834) and create the five spokes for the roses using a 3 gauge needle.

5. Weave your roses with ROSE WHEEL STITCH using six strands of the same colour. Keep these weaving stitches loose throughout your stitching to stop them looking loopy and messy. Make sure not to catch your needle in the anemones.

6. Now, stitch the large pink dahlias using no outline SATIN STITCH. Taking three strands of pink thread (151) and a 5 gauge needle, start each petal in the centre of your marked outline and then working outwards to stitch the sides. Stitch one petal at a time, so when the whole flower is complete, you can still see definition between each petal. Keep your stitches tight and close together so that are no gaps where you can see the underlying fabric. If you see gaps, simply go back and fill them in.

7. Once the dahlias are completely stitched, take three strands of very light shell pink (224) and light rosewood (3859) thread and create long BASIC STITCHes to make the flowers pop. Start by bringing your needle up in the middle of the petal and then back down at the base of the flower. Keep these tight and alternate between the two colours so that all the

base petals have both colours.

8. Next, stitch the billy balls with three strands of medium topaz (783). Create small FRENCH KNOTs by wrapping your thread around the needle twice. Keep these tight and close together.

9. Stitch the orange amaranthus by alternating between three strands of copper (921) and medium golden brown (976) thread. Use FRENCH KNOT stitch, wrapping your thread around the needle twice. The majority of these knots should be made with the medium golden brown (976) thread, using the copper thread (921) just to add more depth to the amaranthus. You don't want any gaps between them, so keep your knots neat and tidy.

10. Now it's time to create the larger leaves. Alternate between three strands of dark olive green (731), olive green (732) and medium olive green (733) threads. Use the non-outline version of SATIN STITCH and stitch neat leaves. Keep them inside your marked outline, but remember that they should look organic and natural. Make sure to start each leaf with one SATIN STITCH in the centre of your marked outline and then work out from this point. As long as you are bringing up your needle on the marked outline and back down on the marked outline, you're doing it right!

11. Create the smaller leaves with three strands of very dark olive green thread (730). Stitch them in the same way as the larger leaves using long, non-outlined SATIN STITCHes.

12. Now, take three strands of very dark hazelnut

brown thread (869) and stitch all the stems for the outside billy balls and the smaller leaves in BACK STITCH. For the billy balls, connect the base of the ball to the bouquet body with small stitches. For the smaller leaves, do the same, making sure to connect the bases of each leaf together with your small stitches. When you make the larger stems, use the same three strands of thread, but use long BASIC STITCHes. Come up with your needle in the middle of the leaf and back down at the bouquet body. Some of the longer stems for the larger leaves will need to be stitched using BACK STITCH to create the definition you see in the picture. Lastly, stitch the branch for the blue berries, using small BACK STITCHes.

13. Finally, take three strands of light antique blue thread (932) and make small FRENCH KNOTs to create the muted blue berries on the ends of the

branches and mingled throughout them. Wrap your thread around the needle once or twice.

14. Once your piece is complete, rinse the blue marker pen out with cold to lukewarm water and allow the fabric to dry before finishing the hoop. You can finish the hoop in one of four ways: RING STITCH, LAYERING, QUICK CUT, or FOLD+GLUE, as outlined in Chapter Six.

chapter six: finishing your hoop

Once you've completed your embroidery pattern, you can finish it in several different ways. Finishing the hoop showcases your design and makes it look more polished. Here we'll explore the different ways to display your project.

Ring stitching is one of the easiest way to finish off your embroidery hoop and make your project look professional.

Once you have finished your embroidery piece, there are several ways you can finish the hoop. One of my favourite ways to do this is to stain the wooden hoop different shades. My absolute favourite is a dark walnut shade, which adds contrast to the bright colours of the threads.

However, before you do anything you have to take your stitching out of the hoop. If you stitched your piece on the back of the hoop, you will need to invert it so the stitching appears in the front of the hoop frame.

To ensure your stitching is centred back in the middle of the hoop, just make sure you line up the creases in the fabric from the inner hoop with the outer hoop. Keep stretching the fabric tight and screwing the embroidery hoop hardware tight until the stitching is centred and the creases are hidden. Don't worry if you notice there are still blue marker pen marks on your fabric. Just wash the fabric again until it has completely disappeared.

RING STITCH
1. The first finishing technique, is the RING STITCH. This technique is very simple and gets the job done quickly. It might not be the prettiest way to finish your embroidery hoop, but it one of the easiest. Start by trimming down the extra fabric around the outside of the hoop frame, until only a small amount remains. Then, taking a piece of embroidery thread, simply stitch around the extra fabric, pulling the thread tight so that the fabric is pulled tight around the back of the hoop. Once you have stitched around the whole hoop, make sure it's not visible from the front of the hoop and then knot and tie the thread off.

QUICK CUT
2. The second finishing technique is the QUICK CUT and it is also a very quick and easy method to finish your hoop. However, with this technique, you will not be covering the back of your hoop at all. If you want to hide any of the messy stitches in the back of the hoop, this is not the technique you're going

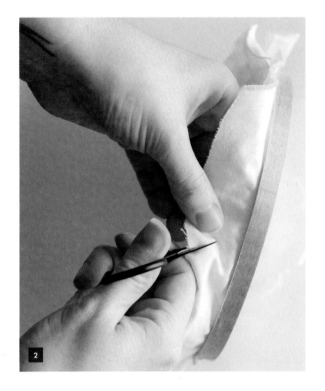

to want to use. Start by screwing the hardware on the hoop as tight as you can to pull the fabric tense in the frame. Check the fabric for any puckers, pulling any of them out, and pulling the fabric even tighter. Once the fabric is as tense as you can make it, simply trim the fabric off at the edge of the hoop frame.

LAYERING

3. The third technique, and the one I use the most often, is called LAYERING. First, start by trimming any thread from the back of your stitching. This is very important, as any excess thread will show through the front of your hoop. Next cut a piece of fabric about the same size as the one you have stitched on. This fabric can be any fabric - linen, cotton, velvet, or even felt. Just choose a light unpatterned material to prevent show through. Once you have selected your fabric, take your stitching and place the two bits of fabric, wrong sides together. Then, put both pieces of fabric

back in the hoop, sandwiched together. Try your best to match the creases in the fabric of your stitching to the hoop frame so you don't have any unsightly marks on the front of your hoop. Then, making sure to pull both the top stitching piece and the bottom backing fabric tight, screw the top hardware of the hoop tight, making sure there are no puckers in the fabric. Once both layers of fabric are pulled tight and there are no bunches in the backing fabric or the top stitching, trim the fabric off the back of the hoop.

FOLD AND GLUE

4. The last hoop finishing technique is called the FOLD+GLUE technique. For this technique, you'll need to firstly make sure there are no thread tails showing on the back of your stitching. Trim any extra threads away from the back. You don't want these showing through the front.

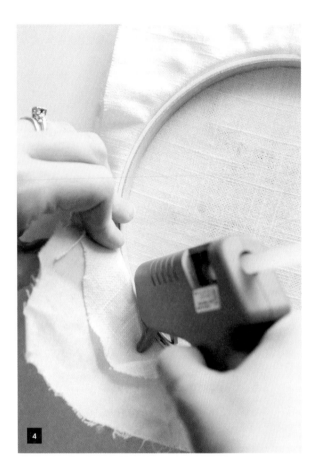

Next, you will need to cut a piece of either felt or quilting flannel in a light coloured shade. Make sure the piece is roughly the same size as your stitching. Now, sandwich the two pieces of fabric together, putting the wrong sides together, as you did in the previous technique. Place it all back in the hoop and make sure both layers are tight and the hardware at the top of the hoop is screwed tight. Next, trim both layers of extra fabric until you have about 3cm of fabric left on the back of the hoop. Using craft or hot glue, fold over the extra fabric around the inside hoop and glue to the hoop. Do not let the glue touch your backing fabric.

Now that your design is finished and attached firmly to its hoop, feel free to decorate with them or give them away as gifts. They also look adorable leaned up on a bookshelf or above the kitchen sink. You can also hang them on walls or lean them up on countertops.

chapter seven: create your own

"We are such stuff
As dreams are made on; and our little life
Is rounded with a sleep."

The Tempest, William Shakespeare

Colour is an integral part of designing patterns. From thread, to fabric, to even the stain you use on the wooden hoops, make sure you have a vision for your design before you start.

You've done it! You've created some amazing pieces and should be really proud of yourself. I hope this book has sparked a passion for the art of embroidery. Now you are ready to create your own floral embroidery patterns. This is where you discover what inspires you, the colours that spark joy in your life, the things that make your creative soul sing, and put them together to create your own beautiful pieces.

When I start working on a pattern, I always start with a quote, a colour palette, the pattern itself or a memory that speaks to me. Pick something that matters to you. A favourite author's quote perhaps? The colours of your childhood bedroom. The flowers that grow in your garden. That's your start point. Once I have got my inspiration, I roughly sketch out my ideas on a drawing pad or iPad, thinking about how my design might translate to an embroidery hoop. Then I start thinking about the colour palette. With botanicals you need to think about whether you want your piece to be muted or bold. You need to focus on the feelings you want to evoke and what colours lie in the spirit of the flowers or plants you are designing with. When choosing colours, think too about the colour of the fabric you are going to use. I have used white in this book, but I love mustard yellow and muted pink linens too.

Next, decide what fabric you are going to use. I love linen for it's natural rustic qualities, but you might like the smoother more refined texture of cotton or even the luxurious look of velvet. A word of warning though - velvet is hard to trace on!

The final part of the design process is to choose your stitches. To create depth and texture, make sure you use French Knots or Rose Wheel Stitches. To create a really 3-D effect, use them both together as I did in the Spring Floral Arrangement. If you want your design to look natural and organic, use the non-outlined version of Satin Stitch to create the leaves. Don't forget, if there are gaps between your leaves and flowers, French Knots are always there to save the day.

Have fun...

chapter three: basic

A simple design using just three shades of green and three easy embroidery stitches. A great beginner project, master this before moving on to the more complex projects in this book.

simple leaves & stems

6 inches

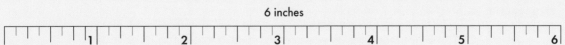

chapter three: basic

Build on your basic embroidery skills and add more colours to your project with this pretty design.
To make the sprays of berries, you will need to master French Knots.

rosemary sprig arrangement

6 inches

chapter three: basic

This beautiful winter rose project in a soft muted colour palette is deceptively easy.
You'll need to learn how to embroider rose wheel stitches to create the flowers.

winter roses

6 inches

chapter four: detailed

With a pretty springtime palette of colours, this project has been created with space around
the design for you to add your own quotation to make it really personal to you.

spring floral arrangement

6 inches

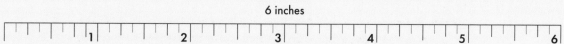

chapter four: detailed

This modern autumnal design uses a non-outlined version of satin stitch
to create a more organic and natural feel to your stitching.

autumnal bouquet

6 inches

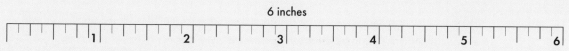

chapter four: detailed

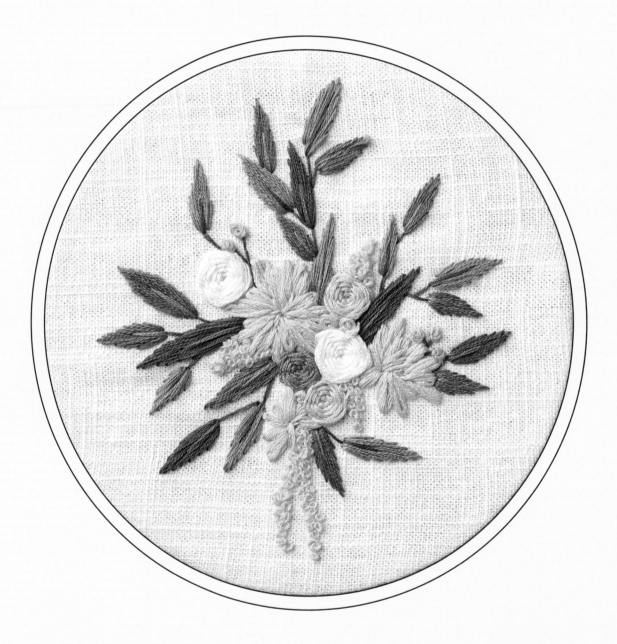

Inspired by the peach, orange and strawberry flavoured sherbet of my childhood, the colour palette was the starting point of this pretty summery design which teaches you lazy daisy stitch.

sherbet bouquet

6 inches

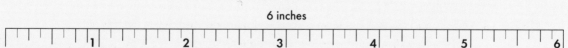

chapter four: detailed

For this piece, I chose the colours before I even started working on the design.
I wanted to use rich gem tones to create a dramatic regal feel.

gem tone bouquet

6 inches

chapter five: intricate

One of the prettiest summery designs, this pattern is inspired by the peonies and roses of my childhood garden. Lots of mixed stitches and a large range of colours makes this a challenging, but fun, project.

spring blooms bouquet

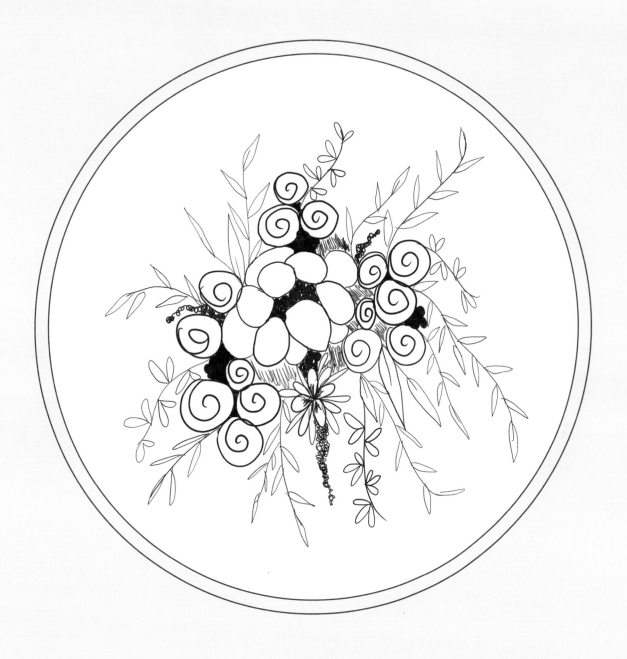

6 inches

| 1 | 2 | 3 | 4 | 5 | 6 |

chapter five: intricate

This piece captures the magic of A Midsummer Night's Dream with a myriad of pastel colours and a combination of many different stitches. It is one of my favourite designs.

midsummer bouquet

6 inches

chapter five: intricate

I have always adored the Halloween colour combination of orange, purple, black and bright green, so I wanted to create a design that could incorporate those colours.

spooky bouquet

6 inches

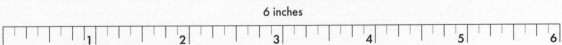

About the author

Teagan Olivia Sturmer is an embroidery artist, author and theatre director inspired by the changing seasons of the Northwoods in America. Hailing from the stormy shores of Lake Superior, Teagan lives with her husband, Brice, and dog, Remus - who loves nothing more than a cuddle when Teagan is stitching or writing. After graduating with a degree in creative writing, Teagan focused her creative skills on hand embroidery. She sells her designs on her Etsy shop, Muted Rose Embroidery, and posts on Instagram @teaganoliviasturmer. She is currently working on a creative novel and directing Shakespeare for her local youth theatre.

Teagan says: "Thank you for joining me on this creative journey. I hope it will be a wonderful learning experience for you and will awaken a passion for stitching. I commend your bravery if you try something new in this book, and I applaud your steadfastness if you are a seasoned stitcher. Good luck on your creative journey, and remember you are made to create. Always create, my friend. I will leave you with this quote."

"If we shadows have offended,
Think but this, and all is mended,
That you have but slumber'd here
While these visions did appear.
And this weak and idle theme,
No more yielding but a dream."

A Midsummer Night's Dream, William Shakespeare

Acknowledgements

Special thanks to my dearest and best, Brice, for your encouragement, support and most importantly, your steadfast love. To Riley, not only are your photographs works of art, but dear friend, so are you. Thank you for believing in me, supporting me and always being there to enjoy a glass of wine. To Lauren, to Ada-Mouse, to Amy, to Ahnna - thank you for your guidance, your counsel, your joy and your love. You have all carried me when I was broken. To the humans of Superior Arts Youth Theater, you are my deepest well of inspiration; thank you for believing in me. To Maggie of Northwoods Flora, thank you for the beautiful flowers and your beautiful spirit. To Alice, Lori, Aileen, Jonathan, Katherine, Jane, Jesse and Jaine who worked on the book for me. Thank you for trusting me with this project and for always being there when I had questions. This has been one of my wildest dreams and you have made it come true.